MY BIBLE STUDY JOURNAL

I, _____

am the owner of the words written in this journal.

Copyright © 2018 by M. Mitch Freeland

All rights reserved.

Published by Kulhanjian's Notebooks & Journals a division of Las Vegas Book Company, Las Vegas, Nevada, U.S.A

Designed by M. Mitch Freeland exclusively for Kulhanjian's Notebooks & Journals

Disclaimer: The publisher and author have used their best efforts in preparing this book; yet they make no representations or warranties to the accuracy or completeness of its contents. Furthermore, the publisher and author disclaim any implied warranties or merchantability or fitness for a particular purpose. The advice and strategies contained in this book may not be suitable for your situation. This book is sold with the understanding that the publisher and author are not engaged in rendering legal, ac-counting, or other professional services. You should consult with a professional. Neither the publisher nor authors shall be liable for any loss of profit or any other commercial damages, including but not limited to special, incidental, consequential, or other damages.

MY BIBLE STUDY JOURNAL
8" x 10"

For information, contact: MMitchFreeland@gmail.com
www.MitchFreeland.com

First Paperback Edition: October 22, 2018

ISBN: 978-172900-5064

SPECIAL DISCOUNT SALES

Books published by Kulhanjian's Notebooks & Journals / Las Vegas Book Company are available at special quantity discounts worldwide to be used for training or for use in promotional programs, thoughtful gifts or for group engaged activities. Quantity discounts are available to Houses of Worship, study groups, corporations, educational institutions and charitable organizations.

Personalized front or back covers and endpapers can be produced in large numbers to meet specific needs.

For information, send us a quick email and tell us what you would like.

Email us at: MMitchFreeland@gmail.com

Table of Contents

Bible Scripture Studied	Date Recorded	Page
How to Use Your Bible Study Journal		5

How to Use Your Bible Study Journal

The Bible is the most important book that has ever been written, because the Bible is the Word of God. When we are reading the Bible, God is speaking to us. When we pray we are speaking to God. When God is speaking to us through the Bible we must give Him our full and undistracted attention.

This journal should be used in conjunction with your Bible. Both your Bible and this journal should be opened together, one beside the other. If you prefer to study the Bible online, you can try WordProject.org, which offers the Bible in over 36 languages for free. On WordProject.org, the English language version of the Holy Bible is available in the King James Version and in the Catholic Version. So, as long as you have a mobile phone, with internet connection, and you have your *Bible Study Journal*, you are equipped to receive God's Word.

Each entry of your *Bible Study Journal* consists of two pages with multiple prompts. There are 49 entries. If you study the Bible once per week you will have filled the journal in just under 12 months. If you plan to study daily, then you will need several journals to cover 12 months worth of study. How often you study is up to you. But, as a Christian, it is better to keep the Word of God with you daily, so daily study is always the best and the quickest way to learn all that the Bible has to offer regarding living a fulfilling Christian life.

Using This Journal
On the first page of your journal you can write your name as the owner of the words written in your journal. Next, you will get to the *Table of Contents*. As you choose a chapter, passage, verse or Book to study, you can record the scripture or the main subject of your study, record the date of study, and page number.

For instruction on how to study the Bible, visit page 104 for a brief overview of methods for studying the Bible.

Beginning With Your First Entry
Fill in the *Date* and *Time*. Fill in the *Place* prompt. If you are studying with others, write down the names of your study partners in the space provided. If studying on your own, check the box, *Solitary Study*.

Next, after you have read the scripture, note it in the space provided. Write down the main subject of the scripture and the persons revealed. If you are not clear about the meaning of what you've read, take your time, pray for understanding and reread the scripture.

Reflect and meditate on the scripture. Reflection is thinking about what you have read. Write down your thoughts. How did you feel as you read the scripture? Write down how you felt in the space provided.

The last two prompts on the first page of your entries asks what the passage teaches you about the Lord and how did the scripture help you today. Be candid when you answer all the questions asked. Remember, this is your journal.

On the second page, you will find more prompts to. Answer each question as thoroughly as you like. There is also a different Bible quote on each of the 44 entry pages.

On the second half of the page there are sentence fill-ins. There are no wrong answers. Example: The first fill-in: I am a _____ person for studying this scripture. You can use the word(s) motivated, inspired, smarter, more caring, concerned, fearless, more loving, etc. You can use one or more words. In the next fill-in, write down what you need to improve. Perhaps you need to be more patient, improve relationships, your focus, etc. In the last fill-in write down the person's name you relate to in the scripture, then write down the reason why. If you want to add more from your thoughts, do so in the *Note* prompt.

The last prompt is that you sign your name to everything you have written. By signing, you are taking ownership and responsibility for your studying. If you were lackluster and your study was a weak attempt, then do not sign. Only sign under deep conviction that you did your best. If you feel you did not do a first rate job, take your time, be patient, and start over. There is no rush. God knows that you are trying and He is with you all the way.

God Bless You and Yours,

M. Mitch Freeland

Date: _____ Time: _____

Place: _____ Study Partners: _____ ☐ Solitary Study

...I am the light of the world. —
John 8:12

Scripture Studied / Who are the persons revealed?
What is the main subject of this scripture?

_____

Reflection of Scripture

_____

I felt _____ **as I read this scripture.**

What does this passage teach me about the Lord?

_____

How did the scripture help me in my life today?

_____

I Am Grateful, Thank You Lord for...

> For God so loved the world, that he gave his only begotten Son, that whosoever believeth in him should not perish, but have everlasting life.
> —John 3:16

Is there instruction for me to follow?

Lord, Lead Me To Become...

Is there a sin to be confessed?

I am a _____ *person for studying this scripture.*

I learned that I need to improve _____

I relate to _____ *in this scripture because* _____

_____

Notes [ ]

I studied with my heart and gave all of myself to the Lord [ ]
Signature

{7}

Date: _____   Time: _____

Place: _____   Study Partners: _____   ☐ Solitary Study

...I am the light of the world. —
John 8:12

Scripture Studied / Who are the persons revealed?
What is the main subject of this scripture?

Reflection of Scripture

I felt _____
_____
as I read this scripture.

What does this passage teach me about the Lord?

How did the scripture help me in my life today?

{8}

I Am Grateful, Thank You Lord for...

> A new commandment I give unto you, That ye love one another; as I have loved you, that ye also love one another. By this shall all men know that ye are my disciples, if ye have love one to another.
> —John 13:34, 35

Is there instruction for me to follow?

Lord, Lead Me To Become...

Is there a sin to be confessed?

I am a _____ *person for studying this scripture.*

I learned that I need to improve _____

I relate to _____ *in this scripture because* _____

Notes

I studied with my heart and gave all of myself to the Lord

Signature

{9}

Date _____ *Time* _____

Place _____ *Study Partners* _____ ☐ *Solitary Study*

...I am the light of the world. —
John 8:12

Scripture Studied / Who are the persons revealed?
What is the main subject of this scripture?

Reflection of Scripture

I felt
_____
_____
as I read this scripture.

What does this passage teach me about the Lord?

How did the scripture help me in my life today?

{10}

I Am Grateful, Thank You Lord for...

> Greater love hath no man than this, that a man lay down his life for his friends.
> —John 15:13

Is there instruction for me to follow?

Lord, Lead Me To Become...

Is there a sin to be confessed?

I am a _____ *person for studying this scripture.*

I learned that I need to improve _____

I relate to _____ *in this scripture because* _____

Notes

I studied with my heart and gave all of myself to the Lord

Signature

Date _____   Time _____

Place _____   Study Partners _____   ☐ Solitary Study

...I am the light of the world. —
John 8:12

Scripture Studied / Who are the persons revealed?
What is the main subject of this scripture?

Reflection of Scripture

I felt
_____
_____
as I read this scripture.

What does this passage teach me about the Lord?

How did the scripture help me in my life today?

I Am Grateful, Thank You Lord for...

[ ]

> ...so that the power of Christ may dwell in me. Therefore I am well content with weaknesses, insults, with distresses, with persecutions, with difficulties, for Christ's sake; for when I am weak, then I am strong.
> —2 Corinthians 12: 9-10

Is there instruction for me to follow?

[ ]

Lord, Lead Me To Become...

[ ]

Is there a sin to be confessed?

[ ]

I am a _____ *person for studying this scripture.*

I learned that I need to improve _____

I relate to _____ *in this scripture because* _____

_____

Notes [ ]

I studied with my heart and gave all of myself to the Lord [ ]

Signature

{13}

Date: _____ Time: _____

Place: _____ Study Partners: _____ ☐ Solitary Study

...I am the light of the world. — John 8:12

Scripture Studied / Who are the persons revealed?
What is the main subject of this scripture?

Reflection of Scripture

I felt
_____
_____
as I read this scripture.

What does this passage teach me about the Lord?

How did the scripture help me in my life today?

{14}

I Am Grateful, Thank You Lord for...

> For I am persuaded, that neither death, nor life, nor angels, nor principalities, nor powers, nor things present, nor things to come, Nor height, nor depth, nor any other creature, shall be able to separate us from the love of God, which is in Christ Jesus our Lord. — Romans 8:38,39

Is there instruction for me to follow?

Lord, Lead Me To Become...

Is there a sin to be confessed?

I am a _____ *person for studying this scripture.*

I learned that I need to improve _____

I relate to _____ *in this scripture because* _____

_____

Notes

I studied with my heart and gave all of myself to the Lord

Signature

{15}

Date　　　　　　　　　　　　Time

Place　　　　　　　Study Partners　☐ Solitary Study

...I am the light of the world. —
John 8:12

Scripture Studied / Who are the persons revealed?
What is the main subject of this scripture?

Reflection of Scripture

I felt
_____
_____
as I read this scripture.

What does this passage
teach me about the Lord?

How did the scripture
help me in my life today?

{16}

I Am Grateful, Thank You Lord for...

> What time I am afraid, I will trust in thee. In God I will praise his word, in God I have put my trust; I will not fear what flesh can do unto me. —Psalms 56:3-4

Is there instruction for me to follow?

Lord, Lead Me To Become...

Is there a sin to be confessed?

I am a _____ *person for studying this scripture.*

I learned that I need to improve _____

I relate to _____ *in this scripture because* _____

Notes

I studied with my heart and gave all of myself to the Lord _____

Signature

{17}

Date Time

Place Study Partners ☐ Solitary Study

...I am the light of the world. —
John 8:12

Scripture Studied / Who are the persons revealed?
What is the main subject of this scripture?

Reflection of Scripture

I felt _____ *as I read this scripture.*

What does this passage teach me about the Lord?

How did the scripture help me in my life today?

{18}

I Am Grateful, Thank You Lord for...

> *I sought the LORD, and he heard me, and delivered me from all my fears.*
> —Psalms 34:4

Is there instruction for me to follow?

Lord, Lead Me To Become...   *Is there a sin to be confessed?*

I am a _____ *person for studying this scripture.*

I learned that I need to improve _____

I relate to _____ *in this scripture because* _____

_____

Notes

I studied with my heart and gave all of myself to the Lord _____
                                                                   Signature

{19}

Date _____   Time _____

Place _____   Study Partners _____   ☐ Solitary Study

...I am the light of the world. — John 8:12

Scripture Studied / Who are the persons revealed?
What is the main subject of this scripture?

Reflection of Scripture

I felt _____ as I read this scripture.

What does this passage teach me about the Lord?

How did the scripture help me in my life today?

I Am Grateful, Thank You Lord for...

> The LORD is my light and my salvation; whom shall I fear? the LORD is the strength of my life; of whom shall I be afraid?.. For in the time of trouble he shall hide me in his pavilion: in the secret of his tabernacle shall he hide me; he shall set me up upon a rock. —Psalms 27:1-5

Is there instruction for me to follow?

Lord, Lead Me To Become...

Is there a sin to be confessed?

I am a _____ *person for studying this scripture.*

I learned that I need to improve _____

I relate to _____ *in this scripture because* _____

_____

Notes

I studied with my heart and gave all of myself to the Lord

Signature

{21}

Date 　　　　　　　　　　　*Time*

Place 　　　　　*Study Partners* ☐ *Solitary Study*

...I am the light of the world. —
John 8:12

Scripture Studied / Who are the persons revealed?
What is the main subject of this scripture?

Reflection of Scripture

I felt
_____
_____
as I read this scripture.

What does this passage teach me about the Lord?

How did the scripture help me in my life today?

{22}

I Am Grateful, Thank You Lord for...

> For the word of God is quick and powerful, and sharper than any two edged sword, piercing even to the dividing asunder of the soul and spirit and of the joins and marrow and is a discerner of the thoughts and intents of the heart. — Hebrews 4:12

Is there instruction for me to follow?

Lord, Lead Me To Become...

Is there a sin to be confessed?

I am a _____ *person for studying this scripture.*

I learned that I need to improve _____

I relate to _____ *in this scripture because* _____

_____

Notes

I studied with my heart and gave all of myself to the Lord

Signature

{23}

Date □   Time □

Place □   Study Partners □   ☐ Solitary Study

...I am the light of the world. —
John 8:12

Scripture Studied / Who are the persons revealed?
What is the main subject of this scripture?

Reflection of Scripture

I felt
_____
_____
as I read this scripture.

What does this passage teach me about the Lord?

How did the scripture help me in my life today?

{24}

I Am Grateful, Thank You Lord for...

> *Study to show thyself approved unto God, a workman that needeth not to be ashamed, rightly dividing the Word of Truth.*
> —2 Timothy 2:15

Is there instruction for me to follow?

Lord, Lead Me To Become...

Is there a sin to be confessed?

I am a _____ *person for studying this scripture.*

I learned that I need to improve _____

I relate to _____ *in this scripture because* _____

_____

Notes

I studied with my heart and gave all of myself to the Lord _____
Signature

{25}

Date _____ *Time* _____

Place _____ *Study Partners* ☐ *Solitary Study*

...I am the light of the world. —
John 8:12

Scripture Studied / Who are the persons revealed?
What is the main subject of this scripture?

Reflection of Scripture

I felt
_____
_____
as I read this scripture.

What does this passage teach me about the Lord?

How did the scripture help me in my life today?

{26}

I Am Grateful, Thank You Lord for...

> In the beginning was the Word, and the Word was with God, and the Word was God. And the Word was made flesh, and dwelt among us, (and we beheld His glory, the glory as of the only begotten of the Father, full of grace and truth.
> —John 1:1-14

Is there instruction for me to follow?

Lord, Lead Me To Become...

Is there a sin to be confessed?

I am a _____ *person for studying this scripture.*

I learned that I need to improve _____

I relate to _____ *in this scripture because* _____
_____

Notes

I studied with my heart and gave all of myself to the Lord

Signature

{27}

Date: _____ Time: _____

Place: _____ Study Partners: _____ ☐ Solitary Study

...I am the light of the world. —
John 8:12

Scripture Studied / Who are the persons revealed?
What is the main subject of this scripture?

Reflection of Scripture

I felt _____ *as I read this scripture.*

What does this passage teach me about the Lord?

How did the scripture help me in my life today?

{28}

I Am Grateful, Thank You Lord for...

> *The LORD is good unto them that wait for him, to the soul that seeketh him. It is good that a man should both hope and quietly wait for the salvation of the LORD.* — Lamentations 3:25-26

Is there instruction for me to follow?

Lord, Lead Me To Become...

Is there a sin to be confessed?

I am a _____ *person for studying this scripture.*

I learned that I need to improve _____

I relate to _____ *in this scripture because* _____

___

Notes

I studied with my heart and gave all of myself to the Lord

Signature

{29}

Date Time

Place Study Partners ☐ Solitary Study

...I am the light of the world. —
John 8:12

Scripture Studied / Who are the persons revealed?
What is the main subject of this scripture?

Reflection of Scripture

I felt
_____
_____
as I read this scripture.

What does this passage teach me about the Lord?

How did the scripture help me in my life today?

{30}

I Am Grateful, Thank You Lord for...

> *Blessed is the man that trusteth in the LORD, and whose hope the LORD is. For he shall be as a tree planted by the waters, and that spreadeth out her roots by the river, and shall not see when heat cometh, but her leaf shall be green; and shall not be careful in the year of drought, neither shall cease from yielding fruit.—Jeremiah 17:7-8*

Is there instruction for me to follow?

Lord, Lead Me To Become...

Is there a sin to be confessed?

I am a _____ *person for studying this scripture.*

I learned that I need to improve _____

I relate to _____ *in this scripture because* _____

_____

Notes

I studied with my heart and gave all of myself to the Lord

Signature

Date [ ] Time [ ]

Place [ ] Study Partners [ ] ☐ Solitary Study

...I am the light of the world. —
John 8:12

Scripture Studied / Who are the persons revealed?

What is the main subject of this scripture?

Reflection of Scripture

I felt _____
_____
as I read this scripture.

What does this passage teach me about the Lord?

How did the scripture help me in my life today?

I Am Grateful, Thank You Lord for...

> In returning and rest shall ye be saved; in quietness and in confidence shall be your strength: and ye would not.
> —Isaiah 30:15

Is there instruction for me to follow?

Lord, Lead Me To Become...

Is there a sin to be confessed?

I am a _____ *person for studying this scripture.*

I learned that I need to improve _____

I relate to _____ *in this scripture because* _____

_____

Notes

I studied with my heart and gave all of myself to the Lord _____
Signature

{33}

Date ____ Time ____

Place ____ Study Partners ____ ☐ Solitary Study

...I am the light of the world. — John 8:12

Scripture Studied / Who are the persons revealed?
What is the main subject of this scripture?

Reflection of Scripture

I felt ____
____
as I read this scripture.

What does this passage teach me about the Lord?

How did the scripture help me in my life today?

{34}

I Am Grateful, Thank You Lord for...

> *Trust in him at all times; ye people, pour out your heart before him: God is a refuge for us.*
> —Psalms 62:8

Is there instruction for me to follow?

Lord, Lead Me To Become...

Is there a sin to be confessed?

I am a _____ *person for studying this scripture.*

I learned that I need to improve _____

I relate to _____ *in this scripture because* _____

Notes

I studied with my heart and gave all of myself to the Lord _____
Signature

{35}

Date ____   Time ____

Place ____   Study Partners ____   ☐ Solitary Study

...I am the light of the world. —
John 8:12

Scripture Studied / Who are the persons revealed?
What is the main subject of this scripture?

Reflection of Scripture

I felt ____
____
as I read this scripture.

What does this passage teach me about the Lord?

How did the scripture help me in my life today?

{36}

I Am Grateful, Thank You Lord for...

And all things, whatsoever ye shall ask in prayer, believing, ye shall receive.
—Matthew 21:22

Is there instruction for me to follow?

Lord, Lead Me To Become...

Is there a sin to be confessed?

I am a _____ *person for studying this scripture.*

I learned that I need to improve _____

I relate to _____ *in this scripture because* _____

_____

Notes

I studied with my heart and gave all of myself to the Lord

Signature

{37}

Date Time

Place Study Partners ☐ Solitary Study

...I am the light of the world. —
John 8:12

Scripture Studied / Who are the persons revealed?
What is the main subject of this scripture?

Reflection of Scripture

I felt
_____
_____
as I read this scripture.

What does this passage teach me about the Lord?

How did the scripture help me in my life today?

{38}

I Am Grateful, Thank You Lord for...

> *If ye then, being evil, know how to give good gifts unto your children, how much more shall your Father which is in heaven give good things to them that ask him?*
> —Matthew 7:11

Is there instruction for me to follow?

Lord, Lead Me To Become...

Is there a sin to be confessed?

I am a _____ *person for studying this scripture.*

I learned that I need to improve _____

I relate to _____ *in this scripture because* _____

_____

Notes

I studied with my heart and gave all of myself to the Lord _____
Signature

{39}

Date _____ Time _____

Place _____ Study Partners _____ ☐ Solitary Study

...I am the light of the world.—
John 8:12

Scripture Studied / Who are the persons revealed?
What is the main subject of this scripture?

Reflection of Scripture

I felt _____
_____
as I read this scripture.

What does this passage teach me about the Lord?

How did the scripture help me in my life today?

I Am Grateful, Thank You Lord for...

> Ask, and it shall be given you; seek, and ye shall find; knock, and it shall be opened unto you: For every one that asketh receiveth; and he that seeketh findeth; and to him that knocketh it shall be opened.
> —Matthew 7:7-8

Is there instruction for me to follow?

Lord, Lead Me To Become...

Is there a sin to be confessed?

I am a _____ *person for studying this scripture.*

I learned that I need to improve _____

I relate to _____ *in this scripture because* _____

_____

Notes

I studied with my heart and gave all of myself to the Lord _____

Signature

{41}

Date _____ Time _____

Place _____ Study Partners _____ ☐ Solitary Study

...I am the light of the world. —
John 8:12

Scripture Studied / Who are the persons revealed?
What is the main subject of this scripture?

Reflection of Scripture

I felt
_____
_____
as I read this scripture.

What does this passage teach me about the Lord?

How did the scripture help me in my life today?

{42}

I Am Grateful, Thank You Lord for...

> But seek ye first the kingdom of God, and his righteousness; and all these things shall be added unto you.
> —Matthew 6:33

Is there instruction for me to follow?

Lord, Lead Me To Become...

Is there a sin to be confessed?

I am a _____ person for studying this scripture.

I learned that I need to improve _____

I relate to _____ in this scripture because _____

_____

Notes

I studied with my heart and gave all of myself to the Lord _____
                                                                Signature

Date:

Time:

Place:

Study Partners: ☐ Solitary Study

...I am the light of the world. — John 8:12

Scripture Studied / Who are the persons revealed?
What is the main subject of this scripture?

Reflection of Scripture

I felt _____ as I read this scripture.

What does this passage teach me about the Lord?

How did the scripture help me in my life today?

{44}

I Am Grateful, Thank You Lord for...

> *And I will make them and the places round about my hill a blessing; and I will cause the shower to come down in his season; there shall be showers of blessing.*
> —Ezekiel 34:26

Is there instruction for me to follow?

Lord, Lead Me To Become...

Is there a sin to be confessed?

I am a _____ *person for studying this scripture.*

I learned that I need to improve _____

I relate to _____ *in this scripture because* _____

_____

Notes

I studied with my heart and gave all of myself to the Lord

Signature

{45}

Date _____ *Time* _____

Place _____ *Study Partners* _____ ☐ *Solitary Study*

...I am the light of the world. —
John 8:12

Scripture Studied / Who are the persons revealed?
What is the main subject of this scripture?

Reflection of Scripture

I felt
_____
_____
as I read this scripture.

What does this passage teach me about the Lord?

How did the scripture help me in my life today?

{46}

I Am Grateful, Thank You Lord for...

> *If ye be willing and obedient, ye shall eat the good of the land, But if ye refuse and rebel, ye shall be devoured with the sword: for the mouth of the LORD hath spoken it.*
> —Isaiah 1:19-20

Is there instruction for me to follow?

Lord, Lead Me To Become...

Is there a sin to be confessed?

I am a _____ *person for studying this scripture.*

I learned that I need to improve _____

I relate to _____ *in this scripture because* _____

_____

Notes

I studied with my heart and gave all of myself to the Lord

Signature

{47}

Date □   Time □

Place   Study Partners   □ Solitary Study

□   □

...I am the light of the world. —
John 8:12

Scripture Studied / Who are the persons revealed?
What is the main subject of this scripture?

Reflection of Scripture

I felt
_____
_____
as I read this scripture.

What does this passage
teach me about the Lord?

How did the scripture
help me in my life today?

{48}

I Am Grateful, Thank You Lord for...

> Thou shalt not be afraid for the terror by night; nor for the arrow that flieth by day; Nor for the pestilence that walketh in darkness; nor for the destruction that wasteth at noonday.
> —Psalms 91:5-6

Is there instruction for me to follow?

Lord, Lead Me To Become...

Is there a sin to be confessed?

I am a _____ *person for studying this scripture.*

I learned that I need to improve _____

I relate to _____ *in this scripture because* _____

_____

Notes

I studied with my heart and gave all of myself to the Lord _____
Signature

{49}

Date   [ ]   *Time*   [ ]

Place   *Study Partners*   ☐ *Solitary Study*

...I am the light of the world. —
John 8:12

Scripture Studied / Who are the persons revealed?
What is the main subject of this scripture?

Reflection of Scripture

I felt _____
_____
as I read this scripture.

What does this passage teach me about the Lord?

How did the scripture help me in my life today?

{50}

I Am Grateful, Thank You Lord for...

> When thou liest down, thou shalt not be afraid: yea, thou shalt lie down, and thy sleep shall be sweet.
> —Proverbs 3:24

Is there instruction for me to follow?

Lord, Lead Me To Become...

Is there a sin to be confessed?

I am a _____ *person for studying this scripture.*

I learned that I need to improve _____

I relate to _____ *in this scripture because* _____

_____

Notes

I studied with my heart and gave all of myself to the Lord _____
Signature

Date Time

Place Study Partners ☐ Solitary Study

...I am the light of the world. —
John 8:12

Scripture Studied / Who are the persons revealed?
What is the main subject of this scripture?

Reflection of Scripture

I felt
_____
_____
as I read this scripture.

What does this passage teach me about the Lord?

How did the scripture help me in my life today?

I Am Grateful, Thank You Lord for...

> Say to them that are of a fearful heart, Be strong, fear not: behold, your God will come with vengeance, even God with a recompence; he will come and save you.
> —Isaiah 35:4

Is there instruction for me to follow?

Lord, Lead Me To Become...

Is there a sin to be confessed?

I am a _____ *person for studying this scripture.*

I learned that I need to improve _____

I relate to _____ *in this scripture because* _____

_____

Notes

I studied with my heart and gave all of myself to the Lord

Signature

Date _____   *Time* _____

Place   *Study Partners*   ☐ *Solitary Study*

...I am the light of the world. —
John 8:12

Scripture Studied / Who are the persons revealed?
What is the main subject of this scripture?

Reflection of Scripture

I felt
_____
_____
as I read this scripture.

What does this passage teach me about the Lord?

How did the scripture help me in my life today?

{54}

I Am Grateful, Thank You Lord for...

> *Fear thou not; for I am with thee: be not dismayed; for I am thy God: I will strengthen thee; yea, I will help thee; yea, I will uphold thee with the right hand of my righteousness.*
> —Isaiah 41:10

Is there instruction for me to follow?

Lord, Lead Me To Become...

Is there a sin to be confessed?

I am a _____ *person for studying this scripture.*

I learned that I need to improve _____

I relate to _____ *in this scripture because* _____

_____

Notes

I studied with my heart and gave all of myself to the Lord _____
Signature

Date: _____ Time: _____

Place: _____ Study Partners: _____ ☐ Solitary Study

...I am the light of the world. — John 8:12

Scripture Studied / Who are the persons revealed?
What is the main subject of this scripture?

_____

Reflection of Scripture

_____

I felt _____ as I read this scripture.

What does this passage teach me about the Lord?

_____

How did the scripture help me in my life today?

_____

I Am Grateful, Thank You Lord for...

> And when thou prayest, thou shalt not be as the hypocrites are: for they love to pray standing in the synagogues and in the corners of the streets, that they may be seen of men. Verily I say unto you, They have their reward.
> —Matthew 6:5

Is there instruction for me to follow?

Lord, Lead Me To Become...

Is there a sin to be confessed?

I am a _____ person for studying this scripture.

I learned that I need to improve _____

I relate to _____ in this scripture because _____

_____

Notes

I studied with my heart and gave all of myself to the Lord _____

Signature

{57}

Date: _____   Time: _____

Place: _____   Study Partners: _____   ☐ Solitary Study

...I am the light of the world. — John 8:12

Scripture Studied / Who are the persons revealed?
What is the main subject of this scripture?

Reflection of Scripture

I felt _____ **as I read this scripture.**

What does this passage teach me about the Lord?

How did the scripture help me in my life today?

I Am Grateful, Thank You Lord for...

> Let us search and try our ways, and turn again to the LORD. Let us lift up our heart with our hands unto God in the heavens. — Lamentations 3:40-41

Is there instruction for me to follow?

Lord, Lead Me To Become...

Is there a sin to be confessed?

I am a _____ person for studying this scripture.

I learned that I need to improve _____

I relate to _____ in this scripture because _____

_____

Notes

I studied with my heart and gave all of myself to the Lord _____

Signature

Date:

Time:

Place:

Study Partners:

☐ Solitary Study

...I am the light of the world. — John 8:12

Scripture Studied / Who are the persons revealed?
What is the main subject of this scripture?

Reflection of Scripture

I felt _____ as I read this scripture.

What does this passage teach me about the Lord?

How did the scripture help me in my life today?

{60}

I Am Grateful, Thank You Lord for...

> Call unto me, and I will answer thee, and shew thee great and mighty things, which thou knowest not.
> —Jeremiah 33:3

Is there instruction for me to follow?

Lord, Lead Me To Become...

Is there a sin to be confessed?

I am a _____ person for studying this scripture.

I learned that I need to improve _____

I relate to _____ in this scripture because _____

Notes

I studied with my heart and gave all of myself to the Lord _____

Signature

Date Time

Place Study Partners ☐ Solitary Study

...I am the light of the world. —
John 8:12

Scripture Studied / Who are the persons revealed?
What is the main subject of this scripture?

Reflection of Scripture

I felt
_____
_____
as I read this scripture.

What does this passage teach me about the Lord?

How did the scripture help me in my life today?

{62}

I Am Grateful, Thank You Lord for...

> *And it shall come to pass, that before they call, I will answer; and while they are yet speaking, I will hear.*
> —Isaiah 65:24

Is there instruction for me to follow?

Lord, Lead Me To Become...

Is there a sin to be confessed?

I am a _____ person for studying this scripture.

I learned that I need to improve _____

I relate to _____ in this scripture because _____

_____

Notes

I studied with my heart and gave all of myself to the Lord _____
                                                                  Signature

{63}

Date _____ Time _____

Place _____ Study Partners _____ ☐ Solitary Study

...I am the light of the world. —
John 8:12

Scripture Studied / Who are the persons revealed?
What is the main subject of this scripture?

Reflection of Scripture

I felt
_____
_____
as I read this scripture.

What does this passage teach me about the Lord?

How did the scripture help me in my life today?

I Am Grateful, Thank You Lord for...

> With my whole heart have I sought thee: O let me not wander from thy commandments.
> —Psalms 119:10

Is there instruction for me to follow?

Lord, Lead Me To Become...

Is there a sin to be confessed?

I am a _____ *person for studying this scripture.*

I learned that I need to improve _____

I relate to _____ *in this scripture because* _____

_____

Notes

I studied with my heart and gave all of myself to the Lord _____

Signature

{65}

Date

Time

Place

Study Partners ☐ Solitary Study

...I am the light of the world. —
John 8:12

Scripture Studied / Who are the persons revealed?
What is the main subject of this scripture?

Reflection of Scripture

I felt

_____

_____

as I read this scripture.

What does this passage
teach me about the Lord?

How did the scripture
help me in my life today?

I Am Grateful, Thank You Lord for...

> I love the LORD, because he hath heard my voice and my supplications. Because he hath inclined his ear unto me, therefore will I call upon him as long as I live.
> —Psalms 116:1-2

Is there instruction for me to follow?

Lord, Lead Me To Become...

Is there a sin to be confessed?

I am a _____ *person for studying this scripture.*

I learned that I need to improve _____

I relate to _____ *in this scripture because* _____

_____

Notes

I studied with my heart and gave all of myself to the Lord

Signature

{67}

Date

Time

Place

Study Partners ☐ Solitary Study

...I am the light of the world. —
John 8:12

Scripture Studied / Who are the persons revealed?
What is the main subject of this scripture?

Reflection of Scripture

I felt
_____
_____
as I read this scripture.

What does this passage
teach me about the Lord?

How did the scripture
help me in my life today?

I Am Grateful, Thank You Lord for...

> Nevertheless he regarded their affliction, when he heard their cry: And he remembered for them his covenant, and repented according to the multitude of his mercies.
> —Psalms 106:44-45

Is there instruction for me to follow?

Lord, Lead Me To Become...

Is there a sin to be confessed?

I am a _____ *person for studying this scripture.*

I learned that I need to improve _____

I relate to _____ *in this scripture because* _____

_____

Notes

I studied with my heart and gave all of myself to the Lord _____

Signature

Date Time

Place Study Partners ☐ Solitary Study

...I am the light of the world. —
John 8:12

Scripture Studied / Who are the persons revealed?
What is the main subject of this scripture?

Reflection of Scripture

I felt
_____
_____
_____
as I read this scripture.

What does this passage teach me about the Lord?

How did the scripture help me in my life today?

{70}

I Am Grateful, Thank You Lord for...

> O God, thou art my God; early will I seek thee: my soul thirsteth for thee, my flesh longeth for thee in a dry and thirsty land, where no water is;
> —Psalms 63:1

Is there instruction for me to follow?

Lord, Lead Me To Become...

Is there a sin to be confessed?

I am a _____ person for studying this scripture.

I learned that I need to improve _____

I relate to _____ in this scripture because _____

_____

Notes

I studied with my heart and gave all of myself to the Lord _____

Signature

{71}

Date _____ Time _____

Place _____ Study Partners _____ ☐ Solitary Study

...I am the light of the world. — John 8:12

Scripture Studied / Who are the persons revealed?
What is the main subject of this scripture?

Reflection of Scripture

I felt _____
_____
as I read this scripture.

What does this passage teach me about the Lord?

How did the scripture help me in my life today?

I Am Grateful, Thank You Lord for...

> Trust in him at all times; ye people, pour out your heart before him: God is a refuge for us.
> —Psalms 62:8

Is there instruction for me to follow?

Lord, Lead Me To Become...

Is there a sin to be confessed?

I am a _____ *person for studying this scripture.*

I learned that I need to improve _____

I relate to _____ *in this scripture because* _____

_____

Notes

I studied with my heart and gave all of myself to the Lord _____

Signature

{73}

Date ⬚ Time ⬚

Place Study Partners ☐ Solitary Study

...I am the light of the world. —
John 8:12

Scripture Studied / Who are the persons revealed?
What is the main subject of this scripture?

Reflection of Scripture

I felt
_____
_____
as I read this scripture.

What does this passage teach me about the Lord?

How did the scripture help me in my life today?

{74}

I Am Grateful, Thank You Lord for...

> When the waves of death compassed me, the floods of ungodly men made me afraid; The sorrows of hell compassed me about; the snares of death prevented me; In my distress I called upon the LORD, and cried to my God: and he did hear my voice out of his temple, and my cry did enter into his ears.
> —2 Samuel 22:5-7

Is there instruction for me to follow?

Lord, Lead Me To Become...

Is there a sin to be confessed?

I am a _____ person for studying this scripture.

I learned that I need to improve _____

I relate to _____ in this scripture because _____

_____

Notes

I studied with my heart and gave all of myself to the Lord _____

Signature

{75}

Date [ ]　　Time [ ]

Place　　Study Partners　　☐ Solitary Study

...I am the light of the world. —
John 8:12

Scripture Studied / Who are the persons revealed?
What is the main subject of this scripture?

Reflection of Scripture

I felt
_____
_____
as I read this scripture.

What does this passage teach me about the Lord?

How did the scripture help me in my life today?

{76}

I Am Grateful, Thank You Lord for...

> For the love of money is the root of all evil: which while some coveted after, they have erred from the faith, and pierced themselves through with many sorrows.
> —1 Timothy 6:10

Is there instruction for me to follow?

Lord, Lead Me To Become...

Is there a sin to be confessed?

I am a _____ *person for studying this scripture.*

I learned that I need to improve _____

I relate to _____ *in this scripture because* _____

_____

Notes

I studied with my heart and gave all of myself to the Lord _____
Signature

{77}

Date ____   Time ____

Place ____   Study Partners ____   ☐ Solitary Study

...I am the light of the world. — John 8:12

Scripture Studied / Who are the persons revealed?
What is the main subject of this scripture?

Reflection of Scripture

I felt _____
_____
as I read this scripture.

What does this passage teach me about the Lord?

How did the scripture help me in my life today?

{78}

I Am Grateful, Thank You Lord for...

> And whatsoever we ask, we receive of him, because we keep his commandments, and do those things that are pleasing in his sight.
> —1 John 3:22

Is there instruction for me to follow?

Lord, Lead Me To Become...

Is there a sin to be confessed?

I am a _____ person for studying this scripture.

I learned that I need to improve _____

I relate to _____ in this scripture because _____

_____

Notes

I studied with my heart and gave all of myself to the Lord _____
Signature

{79}

Date: _____ Time: _____

Place: _____ Study Partners: _____ ☐ Solitary Study

...I am the light of the world. — John 8:12

Scripture Studied / Who are the persons revealed?
What is the main subject of this scripture?

_____

Reflection of Scripture

_____

I felt _____ **as I read this scripture.**

What does this passage teach me about the Lord?

_____

How did the scripture help me in my life today?

_____

{80}

I Am Grateful, Thank You Lord for...

> *Let us therefore come boldly unto the throne of grace, that we may obtain mercy, and find grace to help in time of need.*
> —Hebrews 4:16

Is there instruction for me to follow?

Lord, Lead Me To Become...

Is there a sin to be confessed?

I am a _____ *person for studying this scripture.*

I learned that I need to improve _____

I relate to _____ *in this scripture because* _____

_____

Notes

I studied with my heart and gave all of myself to the Lord _____
Signature

{81}

Date Time

Place Study Partners ☐ Solitary Study

...I am the light of the world. —
John 8:12

Scripture Studied / Who are the persons revealed?
What is the main subject of this scripture?

Reflection of Scripture

I felt
_____
_____
as I read this scripture.

What does this passage
teach me about the Lord?

How did the scripture
help me in my life today?

I Am Grateful, Thank You Lord for...

> But without faith it is impossible to please him : for he that cometh to God must believe that he is, and that he is a rewarder of them that diligently seek him.
> —Hebrews 11:6

Is there instruction for me to follow?

Lord, Lead Me To Become...

Is there a sin to be confessed?

I am a _____ *person for studying this scripture.*

I learned that I need to improve _____

I relate to _____ *in this scripture because* _____

_____

Notes

I studied with my heart and gave all of myself to the Lord _____
Signature

{83}

Date

Time

Place

Study Partners ☐ *Solitary Study*

...I am the light of the world. —
John 8:12

Scripture Studied / Who are the persons revealed?
What is the main subject of this scripture?

Reflection of Scripture

I felt
_____
_____
as I read this scripture.

What does this passage teach me about the Lord?

How did the scripture help me in my life today?

I Am Grateful, Thank You Lord for...

> Praying always with all prayer and supplication in the Spirit, and watching thereunto with all perseverance and supplication for all saints;
> —Ephesians 6:18

Is there instruction for me to follow?

Lord, Lead Me To Become...

Is there a sin to be confessed?

I am a _____ *person for studying this scripture.*

I learned that I need to improve _____

I relate to _____ *in this scripture because* _____

_____

Notes

I studied with my heart and gave all of myself to the Lord _____

Signature

{85}

Date _____   Time _____

Place _____   Study Partners _____   ☐ Solitary Study

...I am the light of the world. —
John 8:12

Scripture Studied / Who are the persons revealed?
What is the main subject of this scripture?

Reflection of Scripture

I felt
_____
_____
as I read this scripture.

What does this passage teach me about the Lord?

How did the scripture help me in my life today?

I Am Grateful, Thank You Lord for...

> *And whatsoever ye shall ask in my name, that will I do, that the Father may be glorified in the Son. If ye shall ask any thing in my name, I will do it.*
> —John 14:13-14

Is there instruction for me to follow?

Lord, Lead Me To Become...

Is there a sin to be confessed?

I am a _____ *person for studying this scripture.*

I learned that I need to improve _____

I relate to _____ *in this scripture because* _____

_____

Notes

I studied with my heart and gave all of myself to the Lord _____

Signature

{87}

Date _____   *Time* _____

Place _____   *Study Partners* _____   ☐ *Solitary Study*

...I am the light of the world. —
John 8:12

Scripture Studied / Who are the persons revealed?
What is the main subject of this scripture?

Reflection of Scripture

I felt
_____
_____
as I read this scripture.

What does this passage teach me about the Lord?

How did the scripture help me in my life today?

{88}

I Am Grateful, Thank You Lord for...

> *Therefore I say unto you, What things soever ye desire, when ye pray, believe that ye receive them, and ye shall have them.*
> —Mark 11:24

Is there instruction for me to follow?

Lord, Lead Me To Become...

Is there a sin to be confessed?

I am a _____ *person for studying this scripture.*

I learned that I need to improve _____

I relate to _____ *in this scripture because* _____

_____

Notes

I studied with my heart and gave all of myself to the Lord _____

Signature

{89}

Date: _____   Time: _____

Place: _____   Study Partners: _____   ☐ Solitary Study

...I am the light of the world. —
John 8:12

Scripture Studied / Who are the persons revealed?
What is the main subject of this scripture?

Reflection of Scripture

I felt _____ as I read this scripture.

What does this passage teach me about the Lord?

How did the scripture help me in my life today?

I Am Grateful, Thank You Lord for...

> But thou, when thou prayest, enter into thy closet, and when thou hast shut thy door, pray to thy Father which is in secret; and thy Father which seeth in secret shall reward thee openly. But when ye pray, use not vain repetitions, as the heathen do: for they think that they shall be heard for their much speaking. — Matthew 6:6-7

Is there instruction for me to follow?

Lord, Lead Me To Become...

Is there a sin to be confessed?

I am a _____ *person for studying this scripture.*

I learned that I need to improve _____

I relate to _____ *in this scripture because* _____

_____

Notes

I studied with my heart and gave all of myself to the Lord _____

Signature

Date: _____ Time: _____

Place: _____ Study Partners: _____ ☐ Solitary Study

...I am the light of the world. —
John 8:12

Scripture Studied / Who are the persons revealed?
What is the main subject of this scripture?

Reflection of Scripture

I felt _____ as I read this scripture.

What does this passage teach me about the Lord?

How did the scripture help me in my life today?

{92}

I Am Grateful, Thank You Lord for…

> Therefore I say unto you, What things soever ye desire, when ye pray, believe that ye receive them, and ye shall have them.
> —Mark 11:24

Is there instruction for me to follow?

Lord, Lead Me To Become…

Is there a sin to be confessed?

I am a _____ person for studying this scripture.

I learned that I need to improve _____

I relate to _____ in this scripture because _____

Notes

I studied with my heart and gave all of myself to the Lord _____
Signature

{93}

Date

Time

Place

Study Partners ☐ Solitary Study

...I am the light of the world. — John 8:12

Scripture Studied / Who are the persons revealed?

What is the main subject of this scripture?

Reflection of Scripture

I felt
_____
_____
as I read this scripture.

What does this passage teach me about the Lord?

How did the scripture help me in my life today?

{94}

I Am Grateful, Thank You Lord for...

> And whatsoever ye shall ask in my name, that will I do, that the Father may be glorified in the Son. If ye shall ask any thing in my name, I will do it.
> —John 14:13-14

Is there instruction for me to follow?

Lord, Lead Me To Become...

Is there a sin to be confessed?

I am a _____ person for studying this scripture.

I learned that I need to improve _____

I relate to _____ in this scripture because _____

_____

Notes

I studied with my heart and gave all of myself to the Lord _____

Signature

{95}

Date Time

Place Study Partners ☐ Solitary Study

...I am the light of the world. —
John 8:12

Scripture Studied / Who are the persons revealed?
What is the main subject of this scripture?

Reflection of Scripture

I felt

_____

_____

as I read this scripture.

What does this passage
teach me about the Lord?

How did the scripture
help me in my life today?

I Am Grateful, Thank You Lord for...

> For thus saith the Lord GOD, the Holy One of Israel; In returning and rest shall ye be saved; in quietness and in confidence shall be your strength: and ye would not.
> —Isaiah 30:15

Is there instruction for me to follow?

Lord, Lead Me To Become...

Is there a sin to be confessed?

I am a _____ *person for studying this scripture.*

I learned that I need to improve _____

I relate to _____ *in this scripture because* _____

_____

Notes

I studied with my heart and gave all of myself to the Lord _____

Signature

{97}

Date Time

Place Study Partners ☐ Solitary Study

...I am the light of the world. —
John 8:12

Scripture Studied / Who are the persons revealed?
What is the main subject of this scripture?

Reflection of Scripture

I felt
_____
_____
as I read this scripture.

What does this passage teach me about the Lord?

How did the scripture help me in my life today?

{98}

I Am Grateful, Thank You Lord for...

> Cause me to hear thy lovingkindness in the morning; for in thee do I trust: cause me to know the way wherein I should walk; for I lift up my soul unto thee.
> —Psalms 143:8

Is there instruction for me to follow?

Lord, Lead Me To Become...

Is there a sin to be confessed?

I am a _____ person for studying this scripture.

I learned that I need to improve _____

I relate to _____ in this scripture because _____

_____

Notes

I studied with my heart and gave all of myself to the Lord _____

Signature

{99}

Date

Time

Place

Study Partners ☐ *Solitary Study*

...I am the light of the world. —
John 8:12

Scripture Studied / Who are the persons revealed?
What is the main subject of this scripture?

Reflection of Scripture

I felt
_____
_____
as I read this scripture.

What does this passage teach me about the Lord?

How did the scripture help me in my life today?

{100}

I Am Grateful, Thank You Lord for...

> Blessed is the man whose strength is in thee; in whose heart are the ways of them. They go from strength to strength.
> —Psalms 84:5-7

Is there instruction for me to follow?

Lord, Lead Me To Become...

Is there a sin to be confessed?

I am a _____ *person for studying this scripture.*

I learned that I need to improve _____

I relate to _____ *in this scripture because* _____

_____

Notes

I studied with my heart and gave all of myself to the Lord _____
Signature

{101}

Date: _____ Time: _____

Place: _____ Study Partners: _____ ☐ Solitary Study

...I am the light of the world. — John 8:12

Scripture Studied / Who are the persons revealed?
What is the main subject of this scripture?

_____

Reflection of Scripture

_____

I felt _____ *as I read this scripture.*

What does this passage teach me about the Lord?

How did the scripture help me in my life today?

{102}

I Am Grateful, Thank You Lord for...

> *I have no greater joy than to hear that my children walk in truth.*
> —3 John 1:4

Is there instruction for me to follow?

Lord, Lead Me To Become...

Is there a sin to be confessed?

I am a _____ *person for studying this scripture.*

I learned that I need to improve _____

I relate to _____ *in this scripture because* _____

_____

Notes

I studied with my heart and gave all of myself to the Lord _____

Signature

{103}

How to Study the Bible

There are many ways to study the Bible. The Bible is many books in one, with one *great purpose*: to reveal the living Word of God, the Lord Jesus Christ (John 1:1-18)

Devotional Bible study is "reading and studying the Word of God in order that we may hear God's voice personally and that we may know how to do His will and to live a better Christian life." (*Holy Bible Family Reference Edition KJV* 1971, pg. 1086, Royal Pub.)

Dr. Howard A. Kelley said: "The best way to study the Bible is to read it daily with close attention and with prayer to see the light that shines from its pages, to meditate upon it, and to continue to read it until somehow it works itself, its words, its expressions, its teachings, its habits of thought, and its presentation of God and His Christ into...one's being"

How Do You Begin?

1) Begin with a prayer
2) Take notes of what you read
3) Read a passage slowly and ask yourself what the passage is about

Ask yourself these questions:

- What is the main subject of the passage?
- Who is writing or speaking and to whom?
- When does this take place?
- Where does this take place?
- Why does the author write the passage?
- What is the key verse of the passage?
- How does the passage fit in within the context?
- How does this passage teach me about the Lord?
- Is there sin for me to confess from this passage?
- Is there a command for me to obey?
- Is there a promise for me to claim?
- Is there instruction for me to follow?
- Is there a prayer I should pray?

Write down in your journal and take notes as you read, and after reading the passage. Read the passage a second time to firm up your answers and to gain deeper insight.

Memorization

It is good to memorize many verses or passages. For instance, you should memorize the Lord's Prayer. You might also want to memorize verses that speak to you more personally—verses that inspire you to live a Christian life.

What is Inductive Bible Study?

Inductive Bible study is applying inductive reasoning as an investigative approach. This is the process of gathering information and then drawing a conclusion. We do this with:

1. **Observation** (What does the passage say? Who, What, Where, When)
2. **Interpretation** (What does the passage mean?)
3. **Application** (How is the passage applied to my life? What does it mean for me personally? How does this truth affect me, my relationship with others, my relationship with God?)

With inductive study you become involved with the Bible on a more intimate level.

You Can Study The Bible Many Ways

- *By Chapters*: There are 1189 Chapters in the Bible. You can study a Chapter a day. In just over three years you will have studied the Bible.
- *By Paragraphs*. What is the main idea? Now rewrite the paragraph in your own words. Read again and rewrite.
- *By Verses*: Break each verse down by separating nouns and verbs for deeper investigation.
- *by Books*: There is the inductive method of study, which was noted. There is also the synthetic method, which entailed the student to read the Book several times until the message /main theme of the Book is clearly revealed.
- *by Words*: Study great words: faith, belief, love, law, etc.
- *by Topics*: Prayers, songs, sermons, God's commands, etc.
- *through Biography*: God reveals Himself to men and through men: The life of Noah, the life of Abraham, etc.

Family Bible Study

Daily family Bible study brings the family together. This is very important for children. Study should be 40-45 minutes. Have a different member begin with a prayer. Read a Chapter. Have each member read a verse from the Chapter. Then ask questions. Every member should have a journal to record the study session. You can also start or finish by everybody singing a hymn

Starting Your Daily Study

You need a routine. Make Bible Study into a good habit. The best time to study is when your mind is fresh and well rested. Setting a study time right after you wake is a good time. Plan to study for 40 to 45 minutes with no breaks or disruptions. Here is how you do it:

- Plan undisturbed time each day
- Write Down your plan and purpose for study. What do you hope to accomplish? With a plan and a purpose you have an objective to achieve.
- Prepare by praying first:
  (*Give me understanding, that I may keep your law and observe it with my whole heart.*—Psalm 119:34). Many prayers are available in Psalm.
- Read slowly and carefully. Do not rush yourself.
- Ask questions while reading
- Turn the scripture into a prayer

A Prayer Journal For Men of Faith

Discover the beauty of our Prayer Journal

- Are you currently studying the Bible?
- Do you belong to a Bible Study Group?
- Do you want to be fully engaged with Bible verse, passages and prayer?
- Do you want to memorialize your thoughts make learning the Bible more fulfilling?
- Are you looking for a special gift for a friend or new Christian?

If you've answered YES to any of these questions, then it sounds like you are ready for the stunning **My Prayer Journal**

Learning the Bible does not have to be difficult. *My Prayer Journal* makes it easier.

Writing down your thoughts in a Prayer Journal is rewarding experience, filled with endless benefits. Knowledge of our Lord cannot be measured, since it is infinite, but we have the book that He wrote.

Here's what you get with your Prayer Journal

- 108 pages
- A Table of Contents for you to fill in with Bible Verse or Passage, Date Recorded and Page
- 97 Entry pages (over 3 months) to record verses, passages, prayers and thoughts

In the Journal there are dedicated spaces for:
- Date
- Bible Verse or Passage
- Command to Be Obeyed
- My Prayer
- Lord, Lead Me to Become...
- What Does This Verse or Passage Teach Me?
- I Love You Lord. Thank You For...

This Journal is the perfect size and style for recording your Prayers and Bible study whether in group study or quiet solitary study. Great for travel and to take with you wherever you go: to the park, beach, hotel, airplane, bus, car, classroom, library, study, kitchen table or bed.

- Size: 8" x 10"
- High quality cream paper
- Premium Matte Cover, flexible and durable
- Perfect bound paperback

My Prayer Journal is perfect for:

- Gifts for Christians
- Family worship--Bible Study reflection
- Kids and Teen Bible and Prayer journaling
- New Christians
- People who are rediscovering Christianity again
- Bible Study Groups
- Sunday School Classes
- Christians who want a deeper, richer, more fulfilling understanding of the Bible and Christianity, and are willing to spend the time to embrace God wholeheartedly with reflective study and faithful worship.

It's practical. It's economical. It's quality. It's beautifully inspired. It's for you!

Start journaling your Bible Study and Prayers today.

Prayer Journal
For the Man of Faith

Available Now at
Amazon, MitchFreeland.com and Fine Bookstores Everywhere

Did you like this journal? Was this journal helpful?

Would you like to reorder?

Reorder Now at: **www.MitchFreeland.com**

Buy multiple books Direct and SAVE!

A Bible Study Journal makes a thoughtful gift anytime

10 Bible Study Journals for only $65.99
FREE SHIPPING!

Visit us and discover the SAVINGS! It's Worth it.

www.MitchFreeland.com

Thank You
God Bless and See you soon.

M. Mitch Freeland

FOR THE ENTIRE FAMILY

Try All of Our Prayer, Bible Study & Sermon Notes Journals—the perfect complements to your Christian life.

Available Now at

MitchFreeland.com, Amazon, eBay & Fine Bookstores Everywhere

{108}

Made in the USA
Columbia, SC
02 April 2019